Book and CD

Really Easy

90s Hits

G000123970

Wise Publications
London/New York/Paris/Sydney/Copenhagen/Madrid/Tokyo

Contents

Exclusive distributors:
Music Sales Limited
8-9 Frith Street, London W1V 5TZ, England.
Music Sales Pty Limited
120 Rothschild Avenue, Rosebery, NSW 2018, Australia.

Order No. AM957715
ISBN: 0-7119-7936-7
This book © 2000 by Wise Publications

Written by Joe Bennett
Music Processed by The Pitts and
    Digital Music Art
Compiled by Nick Crispin
Edited by Sorcha Armstrong

CD programmed by John Moores
CD recorded by Kester Sims
Guitar preparation by Charlie Chandler at
    Chandler Guitars
All Guitars by Arthur Dick, except tracks 2 & 13,
    by Martin Shellard

Book design by Chloë Alexander
Photographs courtesy of LFI
Introduction photographs by George Taylor

Printed in the United Kingdom by Printwise
    (Haverhill) Limited, Haverhill, Suffolk.

Your Guarantee of Quality
As publishers, we strive to produce every book to the highest commercial standards.

The music has been freshly engraved and the book has been carefully designed to minimise awkward page turns and to make playing from it a real pleasure. Particular care has been given to specifying acid-free, neutral-sized paper made from pulps which have not been elemental chlorine bleached. This pulp is from farmed sustainable forests and was produced with special regard for the environment. Throughout, the printing and binding have been planned to ensure a sturdy, attractive publication which should give years of enjoyment.

If your copy fails to meet our high standards, please inform us and we will gladly replace it.

www.musicsales.com

Music Sales' complete catalogue describes thousands of titles and is available in full colour sections by subject, direct from Music Sales Limited. Please state your areas of interest and send a cheque/postal order for £1.50 for postage to: Music Sales Limited, Newmarket Road, Bury St. Edmunds, Suffolk IP33 3YB.

Introduction

Welcome to Really Easy Guitar, a fantastic new way to learn the songs you love.

This book will teach you how to play 14 classic songs – and you don't even have to be able to read music!

Inside you will find lyrics and chords for each song, complete with the chord shapes you need to start playing immediately. There's a special introduction to each song, with helpful hints and playing tips. Fretboxes and guitar TAB teach you the famous riffs and patterns that everyone will recognise.

The accompanying 14-track CD features professionally recorded soundalike versions of each song – vocals have been left out so that you can sing along.

Just follow the simple four-step guide to using this book and you will be ready to play along with your favourite bands!

1 Tune Your Guitar

Before you can start to play along with the backing tracks, you'll need to make sure that your guitar is in tune with the CD. Track 1 on the CD gives you notes to tune to for each string, starting with the top E string, and then working downwards.

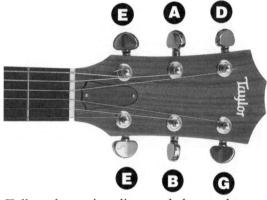

Alternatively, tune the bottom string first and then tune all the other strings to it.

Follow the tuning diagram below and tune from the bottom string upwards.

6th to 5th string	5th to 4th string	4th to 3rd string	3rd to 2nd string	2nd to 1st string

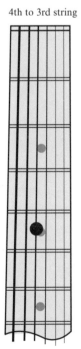

2 Understanding fretbox diagrams

Throughout this book, fretbox diagrams are used to show chord shapes and scale patterns. Think of the box as a view of the fretboard from head on – the thickest (lowest) string is on the left and the thinnest (highest) string is on the left.

The horizontal lines correspond to the frets on your guitar; the circles indicate where you should place your fingers.

An x above the box indicates that that string should not be played; an o indicates that the string should be played open.

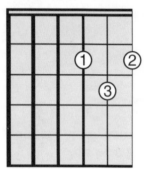

Hence, when playing this chord of D, make sure that you don't hit the bottom two strings.

All the chords you need for each song are given at the top of the song, in the order that they appear in that song.

Am

Am/G

D9/F#

F

Shapes that are played higher up the neck are described in the same way – the lowest fret used is indicated to the left of the box. A curved line above the box shows that a first finger barre should be used.

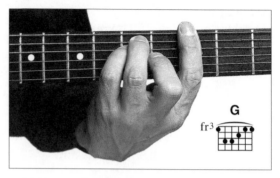

This barre chord of G is played at the third fret, with the first finger stretching across all six strings.

3 Understanding scale patterns

We can also use chord box diagrams to show you certain useful scale patterns on the fretboard. When a box is used to describe a scale pattern, suggested fingerings are also included.

Black circles show you the root note of the scale. If the root note of the scale is an open string, this is indicated by a double circle. Grey circles represent notes of the scale below the lowest root note.

So in this example, the root note of the scale is the open D string, with another D appearing at the third fret on the B string.

4 Understanding TAB

TAB is another easy way to learn the
famous riffs and hooks in each song. The
six horizontal lines represent the six strings
of the guitar – the lowest line represents
the lowest string (low E), while the highest
line represents the highest string (high E).
The number on each line tells you which
fret should be played.

Although we've also included traditional
music notation, you don't actually need to
be able to read music to use TAB – just
listen to the recording and follow the fret
positions on the TAB and you'll soon be
playing along. There are certain special
symbols which are used:

Hammer-on

Look out for a slur connecting two
numbers – when the second number is
higher than the first this is called a
'hammer-on'. Place one finger at the lower
of the two frets indicated and pick that
string, then, without picking the string
again, place your next finger at the higher
fret. You should hear a smooth change in
sound between the two notes.

Pull-off

A pull-off is the opposite of a hammer-on, and is denoted by a slur joining two TAB numbers, where the second number is lower than the first one.

    Place your fingers at the two fret positions indicated, and pick the first (higher) note, then simply lift the top finger, without picking the string again, allowing the bottom note to ring out.

Slide

A slide between two notes is denoted by a short line in the TAB. Simply play the first note, and then move your finger to the new fret position by sliding it along the fretboard, restriking the string as you arrive at the new position.

Legato slide

A legato slide is exactly the same as a normal slide, except that the second note is not picked again.

Bend

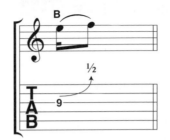

String bends are indicated as shown above – the amount that you need to bend the string is indicated near the arrow and could be ¼ tone (a decorative bend), ½ tone (the equivalent of one fret) or 1 tone (the equivalent of two frets).

Palm Muting

To get this percussive effect, place the side of your picking hand against the strings near the bridge as you pick.

Animal Nitrate

March 1993 No. 7

Note Tune Guitar Down One Semitone

SUEDE'S 3RD SINGLE, back in March 1993, was their biggest hit to date. Whilst previous recordings such as 'Metal Mickey' and 'The Drowners' proved that they were a guitar band to watch, no-one was prepared for Bernard Butler's glam-influenced guitar frenzy in 'Animal Nitrate'.

The track showcases not only his considerable skill as a player, but also his ability to weave lead lines in and out of vocal phrases. Check out the CD recording - there are two guitars, one of which is playing solo lines almost throughout the track. The main riff (see tab) is played under the chorus words "turns you on…" and similar string-skipping lead line ideas are used on the solo.

▼ **D major pentatonic/ B minor pentatonic solo shape**

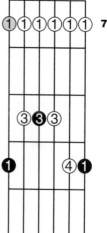

Improvising

Butler often uses pentatonic scales, but in this track he's using alternating minor and major pentatonic ideas in relative keys. The good news for us, of course, is that it means we can improvise over the track using one scale shape throughout! The fretbox shows the B minor/D major pentatonic box shape at the 7th fret, which should be all you need to make up solo lines over the verse or chorus.

How to get that sound

Although we've seen Bernard with various guitars over the years, he's most commonly associated with the Gibson 335 f-hole semi-solid, and if you can approximate the high-output warm tone of a 335's bridge pickup, so much the better. The overdrive on the track is fairly high-gain, so if you're playing a lower-output Strat-type guitar, select the middle pickup and boost the gain or drive control on your amp or pedal. For the real pedal freaks, take a listen to the C chord at the end of the second chorus – there's just a hint of a phaser effect in there.

▼ **Chorus riff**

"There's a definite domestic violence feel to 'Animal Nitrate'. But behind that there's a real sadness and a real feeling that I've always wanted to express."
Brett Anderson

2 Animal Nitrate

Words & Music by Brett Anderson & Bernard Butler

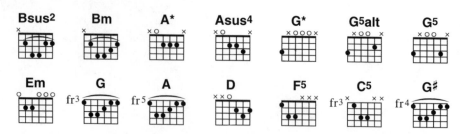

Bsus2   Bm   A*   Asus4   G*   G5alt   G5   Em   G   A   D   F5   C5   G#

Tune guitar down one semitone

Intro

‖: Bsus2 Bm Bsus2 A* Asus4 A* │ G* G5alt G5 Em │ │

│ Bm   A* Asus4 A* │ G   Em   :‖

Verse 1

   Bm A G   Em
Like his dad you know that he's had
Bm A   G Em
Animal nitrate in mind.
      Bm A   G   Em
Oh, in your council home he jumped on your bones,
      Bm A   G
Now you're taking it time after time.

Chorus 1

     A   D G D G
Oh, it turns you on, ___ on, ___
Bm A G
And now he has gone.
       D G D G
Oh, what turns you on, ___ on, ___
Bm   A F5 C5
Now your animal's gone? ___

Verse 1

    Bm A   G   Em
Well he said he'd show you his bed
      Bm   A G Em
And the delights of the chemical smile, ___
      Bm A   G   Em
So in your broken home he broke all your bones,
      Bm A   G
Now you're taking it time after time.

Chorus 2

       A   **D G D G**
Oh, it turns you on, ___ on, ___

Bm   **A**   **G**
And now he has gone.

                D G D G
Oh, what turns you on, ___ on, ___

Bm   **A**   **F5**   **C5**
Now your animal's gone? ___

Solo

| Bm G | G♯ G | Bm G | G♯ G |

| Bm G | G♯ G | Bm G | G♯ G ‖

Chorus 3

  A   **D G D G**
 What does it take to turn you on, ___ on, ___

Bm **A**   **G**
 Now he has gone?

              D   **G D G**
Now you're over twenty one? ___ Oh, ___

Bm   **A**   **G**
Now your animal's gone?

Outro

   (G) D   **G**   **D G**
‖: Animal, he was animal, ___

      Bm A   G
An animal, ___ oh. :‖   *Repeat to fade with vocal ad lib.*

The Day We Caught The Train

June 1996 No. 4

OCEAN COLOUR SCENE, like many guitar bands of the '90s (Pulp, Manic Street Preachers), took a long time to achieve big success. Their first single, back in 1991, only just made the Top 50. It wasn't until their riff-driven 'Riverboat Song' was used in TV show *TFI Friday* that their hard work paid off.

▼ D major scale

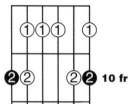

Retro guitars

'The Day We Caught The Train' was their second Top 10 hit, and the band's retro roots were already beginning to show, with the Faces-influenced chord pattern and Mick Ronson-style lead playing. The song uses two rhythm guitars – one electric and one acoustic – plus heavy chord backing from the piano part. This leaves plenty of room on the backing track for improvised soloing – try using the D major scale box shape shown to create your own melodic ideas.

Guitarist and frontman Steve Cradock is most often seen with a Gibson Les Paul Gold Top, but any guitar with a humbucker at the bridge should create the desired effect if you dial in a subtle amount of amp overdrive. Like many of his influences (Ronson, Paul Weller, Pete Townshend), Cradock rarely uses any other effects – there's hardly even reverb on this track.

Fascinating rhythms

To keep the chord parts interesting, try to vary the accompaniment style in the different sections. Start with long, open chords in the first part of each verse, then use sharp, medium-paced downstrokes for the "Rapping on the windows…solid rock" section. Build up with stronger 4-to-the-bar strumming in the pre-chorus, then let rip with big, ringing open chords for the chorus.

There's very little actual lead playing on the track, but as the choruses progress the electric guitar part becomes busier. The tablature shows one of the ideas used around the D-A-G-Em loop of the outro chorus.

▼ Chorus accompaniment riff

3 The Day We Caught The Train

Words & Music by Simon Fowler, Steve Cradock, Oscar Harrison & Damon Minchella

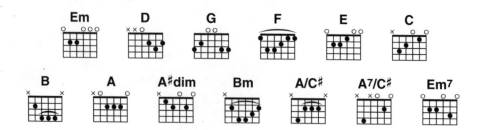

Verse 1

      Em   D   G
I never saw it as the start, it's more a change of heart.
F   E
Rapping on the windows, whistling down the chimney pot.
G   D
Blowing off the dust in the room where I forgot,
   C   **B**
I laid my plans in solid rock.
Em
Stepping through the door like a troubadour,
                A
Whiling just an hour away,
Em   A
Looking at the trees on the roadside, feeling it's a holiday.

Chorus 1

  D   A#dim
You and I should ride the coast
     Bm   A/C#   Em
And wind up in our favourite coats just miles away.
G
  Roll a number, write another song
    A   A7/C#   D
Like Jimmy heard the day he caught the train.
    A   **G**   **Em** **D**
Oh __ la la, oh __ la la,
    A   **G**   **Em7**
Oh __ la la, oh __ la.

Verse 2

Em   D   G
He sipped another rum and coke and told a dirty joke.

F   E
Walking like Groucho, sucking on a Number 10.

G   D
Rolling on the floor with the cigarette burns walked in

     C   B
I'll miss the crush and I'm home again.

Em
Stepping through the door with the night in store,

                        A
Whiling just an hour away.

Em   A
Step into the sky in the starbright, feeling it's a brighter day.

Chorus 2   As Chorus 1

Bridge

A
   You and I should ride the tracks

                                            D
And find ourselves just wading through tomorrow.

A
   And you and I, when we're coming down,

                                          D
We're only getting back, and you know I feel no sorrow.

          A   G   Em7
Spoken: (We've got the whole wide world.)

           | D   A | G   Em7 |
           D   A   G   Em7   D
Sung: Oh ___ la la, oh ___ la la,

                 A   G   Em7   D
           Oh ___ la la, oh ___ la la.

Outro

         D   A
‖:   When you find that things are getting wild,

      G   Em7
Don't you want days like these? :‖ *Play 4 times*

      D   A   G   Em7
‖: Oh ___ la la, oh ___ la la. :‖ *Repeat to fade*

4 Disco 2000

December 1995 No. 7

SHEFFIELD-BASED PULP were 'the' success story of 1995. A magnificent Glastonbury performance shot their album *Different Class* to the UK number 1 slot, and the singles 'Common People' and 'Mis-Shapes' were both Top 10 hits. 'Disco 2000' showed off songwriter Jarvis Cocker's usual urban wit, with twin guitarists Russell Senior and the recently-recruited Mark Webber providing the electric backing.

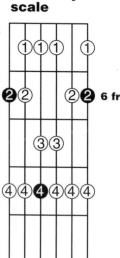

▼ **B♭ major scale**

6 fr

The main riff

The song opens on the Bowie-influenced Fsus4 riff (see tab), which can be moved up five frets to create the B♭ equivalent. The riff isn't difficult, but try to ensure that you don't catch any unwanted open strings, or that muted accompaniment style won't be effective. The chorus accompaniment uses simple melodic lines using the B♭ major scale (see fretbox). On the original it's almost all played by sliding one finger up and down the third (G) string, but we've included the full box shape here in case you want to work on your own melodic ideas.

How to get that sound

The guitar sound is a thick amp overdrive, although it's worth noting that Pulp have been known to double up rhythm parts for a fatter accompaniment sound. Use a middle pickup setting and a fairly heavy overdrive, but back off the volume on the guitar slightly to avoid the whole effect becoming too 'metal'. Try a medium-length room reverb setting but no other effects.

▼ **Intro riff**

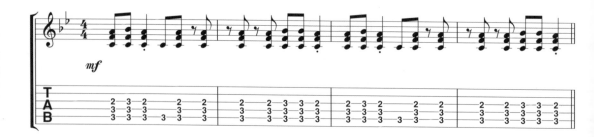

Disco 2000

Words by Jarvis Cocker. Music by Pulp

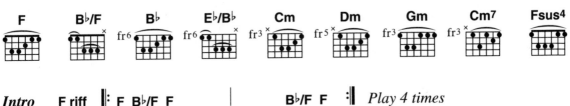

Intro   F riff ‖: F B♭/F F | B♭/F F :‖ *Play 4 times*

B♭ riff ‖: B♭ E♭/B♭ B♭ | E♭/B♭ B♭ :‖

Verse 1

       F riff
Oh, we were born within an hour of each other,

Our mothers said we could be sister and brother,
      B♭ riff
Your name is De-bo-rah, Deborah,

It never suited ya.
    F riff
And they said that when we grew up,

We'd get married and never split up,
     B♭ riff
Oh, we never did it,

Although I often thought of it.

Pre-chorus 1

        Cm
Oh, Deborah, do you recall?

Your house was very small,

With woodchip on the wall,

When I came round to call
       F
You didn't notice me at all.

Disco 2000

Chorus 1

B♭
And I said "Let's all meet up in the year two thousand,
Dm   **Gm**
Won't it be strange when we're all fully grown,

                         Cm⁷   **Fsus⁴** **F**
Be there two o'clock by the fountain down the road."_____
B♭
I never knew that you'd get married,
Dm   **Gm**
I would be living down here on my own,

                        Cm⁷   **Fsus⁴** **F**
On that damp and lonely Thursday years ago. _____

Verse 2

F riff
You were the first girl at school to get breasts,

And Martyn said that you were the best,
                  B♭ riff
Oh, the boys all loved you but I was a mess,

I had to watch them trying to get you undressed.
                F riff
We were friends, _____ that was how it went,

I used to walk you home sometimes but it meant,
                B♭ riff
Oh, it meant nothing to you

'Cause you were so popular.

Pre-chorus 2   As Pre-chorus 1

Chorus 2   As Chorus 1

Instrumental ‖: F B♭/F F | B♭/F F :‖

                      ‖: B♭ E♭/B♭ B♭ | E♭/B♭ B♭ :‖

	Cm
Pre-chorus 3	Oh, Deborah, do you recall?

Your house was very small,

With woodchip on the wall,

When I came round to call

F
You didn't notice me at all.

B♭
Chorus 3   And I said "Let's all meet up in the year two thousand,

Dm   **Gm**
Won't it be strange when we're all fully grown,

              Cm⁷   **Fsus⁴ F**
Be there two o'clock by the fountain down the road."_____

B♭
I never knew that you'd get married,

Dm   **Gm**
I would be living down here on my own,

             Cm⁷   **Fsus⁴ F**
On that damp and lonely Thursday years ago. _____

B♭
Outro   What are you doin' Sunday, baby?

Dm
Would you like to come and meet me, maybe?

Gm   **Cm⁷ Fsus⁴ F**
You can even bring your baby, ooh. _____

B♭
What are you doin' Sunday, baby?

Dm
Would you like to come and meet me, maybe?

Gm   **Cm⁷ Fsus⁴** **F**   **B♭**
You can even bring your baby, ooh, _____ ooh. _____

5 Hand In My Pocket

October 1995 No. 26 (2nd single)

BEFORE 1995, hardly anyone outside her native Canada had heard of Alanis Morissette (and if you take a listen to her first two 'teeny-bop' albums it's fairly easy to understand why!). However, with the release of the album *Jagged Little Pill* in 1995 she became a worldwide star overnight. 'Hand In My Pocket' is one of the most memorable tracks, with its simple vocal hook and eccentric lyrics.

Chord tips

The guitar part isn't at all difficult, consisting as it does of variations on the open chords of G, F and C. Guitarist Glenn Ballard uses an open G5 shape, and plays the other chords whilst maintaining the first and second strings at the third fret, creating the high drone effect that characterises the track. (You can hear a similar effect on Oasis' 'Wonderwall', which was released later that same year). The rhythmic groove hardly varies throughout, so once you've mastered the intro, it's simply a question of moving the chords while the strumming hand pattern stays the same throughout.

How to get that sound

Like much of the album, the song uses a half-distorted/half-clean guitar sound – with this setting, players can vary the amount of overdrive by the way they strike the strings. The tone is fairly bright (use a bridge pickup, and turn the tone pot up full) and there's a short reverb added. Failing that, the whole song should be equally playable on an acoustic.

▼ Basic rhythmic pattern

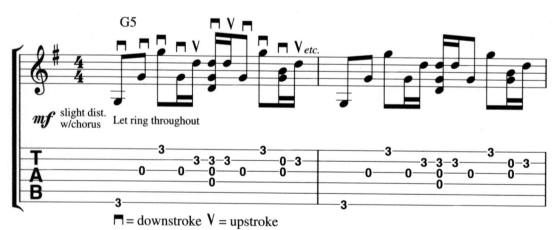

Alanis favours open chord shapes and the same strumming pattern throughout this song: so you should find it fairly simple

5 Hand In My Pocket

Words by Alanis Morissette. Music by Alanis Morissette & Glen Ballard

G5   G5/F   Csus2   G5/D

Intro | G5 | G5 | G5 | G5 ||

Verse 1

G5
I'm broke but I'm happy, I'm poor but I'm kind,

I'm short but I'm healthy, yeah.

I'm high but I'm grounded, I'm sane but I'm overwhelmed,

I'm lost but I'm hopeful baby.

Chorus 1

                               G5/F   Csus2
And what it all comes down to

                       G5
Is that everything's gonna be fine, fine, fine,

               G5/F
'Cause I got one hand in my pocket

         Csus2   G5/D   G5
And the other one is giving a high five.

Verse 2

G5
I feel drunk but I'm sober, I'm young and I'm underpaid,

I'm tired but I'm working, yeah.

I care but I'm restless, I'm here but I'm really gone,

I'm wrong and I'm sorry baby.

Chorus 2

G5/F   Csus2
And what it all comes down to

                       G5
Is that everything's gonna be quite alright,

      G5/F
'Cos I've got one hand in my pocket

      Csus2   G5/D   G5
And the other one is flicking a cigarette.

Solo | G5 | G5 | G5 | G5 | G5 | G5 | G5 | G5 ||

Chorus 3

           G5/F   Csus2
And what it all comes down to

                  G5
Is that I haven't got it all figured out just yet,

      G5/F
'Cos I've got one hand in my pocket

      Csus2   G5/D   G5
And the other one is giving a peace sign.

Verse 3

G5
I'm free but I'm focused, I'm green but I'm wise,

I'm hard but I'm friendly baby.

I'm sad but I'm laughing, I'm brave but I'm chicken shit,

I'm sick but I'm pretty baby.

Chorus 4

           G5/F   Csus2
And what it all boils down to

                 G5
Is that no one's got it figured out just yet.

      G5/F
But I've got one hand in my pocket

      Csus2   G5/D   G5
And the other one is playing a piano.

          G5/F   Csus2
And what it all comes down to my friends

                 G5
Is that every thing is just fine, fine, fine,

      G5/F
'Cos I've got one hand in my pocket

      Csus2   G5/D   G5
And the other one is hailing a taxi cab.

6 Hush

March 1997 No. 2

ALTHOUGH KULA SHAKER'S Crispian Mills is a fine songwriter in his own right, he can't lay any claim to the anthemic "Na na na naaa" chorus that is 'Hush'. The song was written by American solo artist Joe South, and had already been a US Top 5 hit for Deep Purple back in 1968 (if you want to hear the original, check out their debut album *Shades of Deep Purple*).

This '90s version is considerably faster in tempo, but otherwise it's pretty faithful to the original '60s recording, even down to the retro Hammond organ parts. It's largely driven by the chords, so once you've got the hang of the rapid strumming part on the intro (see tab), you should try to maintain that powerful rhythmic style throughout the track. Remember to keep your wrist relaxed!

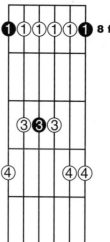

▼ C minor pentatonic soloing shape

How to get that sound

There are two basic guitar sounds on the track. The first one you hear is a fairly clean electric rhythm part, which uses the bridge pickup and a *tiny* bit of amp overdrive. The other is a more distorted lead part, featuring a wah-wah pedal and a fair bit of reverb (if you've got adjustable reverb, set it to 'Hall' mode).

Stolen chords?

Because there are so many sections that dwell on one chord, it's a great track for improvising solos – try the C minor pentatonic scale shape shown in the fretbox. We've recreated Crispian Mills' exact solo on the CD, but feel free to make up your own.

Fascinating fact

The chord sequence is exactly the same (albeit in a different key) as the pattern used in Jimi Hendrix's classic 'Hey Joe'. You can even hear the bassist stealing a few notes from its outro riff here and there…

▼ Rhythmic pattern from intro

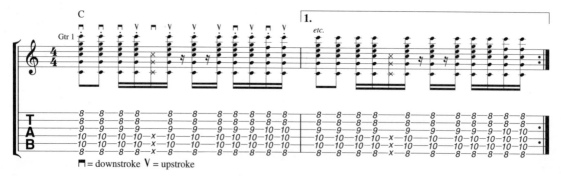

∏ = downstroke V = upstroke

"The whole thing about music isn't necessarily about how good you are, it's about what's driving you to be a musician."
Crispian Mills

15 Hush

Words & Music by Joe South

Chords: C (fr3), Csus4 (fr3), C7#9, A♭ (fr4), E♭ (fr6), B♭, F

Intro

| C Csus4 | C Csus4 | C Csus4 | C   Csus4 |

One, two, three, four.

| C Csus4 | C Csus4 | C Csus4 | C Csus4 |

| C7#9 | C7#9 | C7#9 | C7#9 ||

Link 1

A♭   E♭   B♭   F   C7#9
Na na-na na, na-na na na na,
A♭   E♭   B♭   F   C7#9
Na na-na na, na-na na na na.

Verse 1

                 C
Well, got a silly little girl, she's on my mind,

Look out about, she looks so fine.

She's the best girl that I ever had,

'Cept that's the girl that made me feel so sad.

Link 2

A♭   E♭   B♭   F   C7#9
Na na-na na, na-na na na na,
A♭   E♭   B♭   F   C7#9
Na na-na na, na-na na na na.

Chorus 1

          C7#9   F   B♭
Hey, now, hush, hush I thought I heard you calling my name, now,
C7#9   F   B♭
Hush, hush, you broke my heart, but that was a dream, now.
C7#9   F   B♭
Hush, hush I thought I heard you call my name, now,
C7#9   F   B♭
Hush, hush, you broke my heart, but that was a dream, now.

cont.

C7♯9
Early in the morning, late in the evening,

Oh, gotta believe me, honey,

Oh, I never was a dreamer.

Solo 1 | **C7♯9** | **C** | **C** | **B♭** **F** |

| **C7♯9** | **C7♯9** | **C7♯9** | **B♭** **F** ‖

Chorus 2
C7♯9   **F**   **B♭**
Hush, hush I thought I heard you calling my name, now,
C7♯9   **F**   **B♭**
Hush, hush, you broke my heart, but that was a dream, now.
C7♯9   **F**   **B♭**
Hush, hush I thought I heard you call my name, now,
C7♯9   **F**   **B♭**
Hush, hush, you broke my heart, but that was a dream, now.
C7♯9
Early in the morning, late in the evening, oh _____ yeah!

Solo 2 | **C7♯9** | **C** | **C** | **B♭** **F** |

| **C7♯9** | **C7♯9** | **C** | **B♭** **F** ‖

Link 3
A♭   **E♭**   **B♭**   **F**   **C7♯9**
Na na-na na, na-na na na na,
A♭   **E♭**   **B♭**   **F**   **C7♯9**
Na na-na na, na-na na na na.

Coda
A♭   **E♭**
Na, _____ na-na na, _____
        B♭   **F**   **C7♯9**
Na-na na, _____ na na.

27

7 Motorcycle Emptiness

June 1992 No. 17

'**MOTORCYCLE EMPTINESS**' was taken from the Manics' 1992 debut album *Generation Terrorists*, and it's an excellent example of the band's sound. Singer-guitarist James Dean Bradfield combines sad-angry lyrics with memorable lead guitar lines, and anyone who's spent time in a music shop during the past ten years will have no doubt as to his enduring popularity with guitarists.

The main riff

The track opens with a hammer-on/pull-off lead riff, which is repeated in various forms throughout the track. There are two versions in the tab below – the first is heard at the very start of the song, and is immediately followed by the second. Using these two examples you should be able to get through most of the riffs in the track.

The up-and-down strumming of the rhythm part is broken only on the middle section. Here, you should pick across the barre chord shapes on the second, third and fourth strings, repeating the picking pattern each bar as you change chords. Bradfield's guitar sound is no mystery – that white Les Paul has the bridge pickup selected, and the whole thing goes into a LOUD valve amp. Subtle reverb can be added, but no other effects should be used.

Fascinating fact

The band promised to split up after the *Generation Terrorists* album was released. Good thing for British guitar music that they didn't!

▼ **Riff 1**

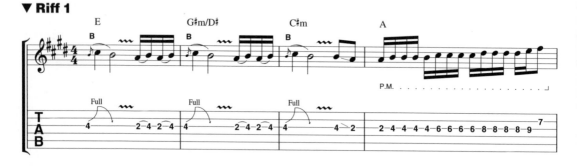

▼ **Riff 2**

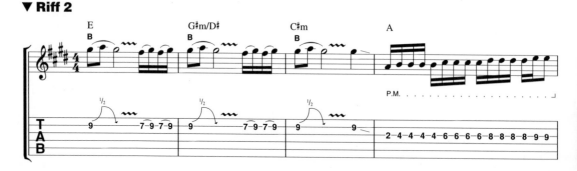

"We thought 'Motorcycle Emptiness' was universal, and I still think it's fantastic."
Nicky Wire

Motorcycle Emptiness

Words by Nicky Wire & Richey James

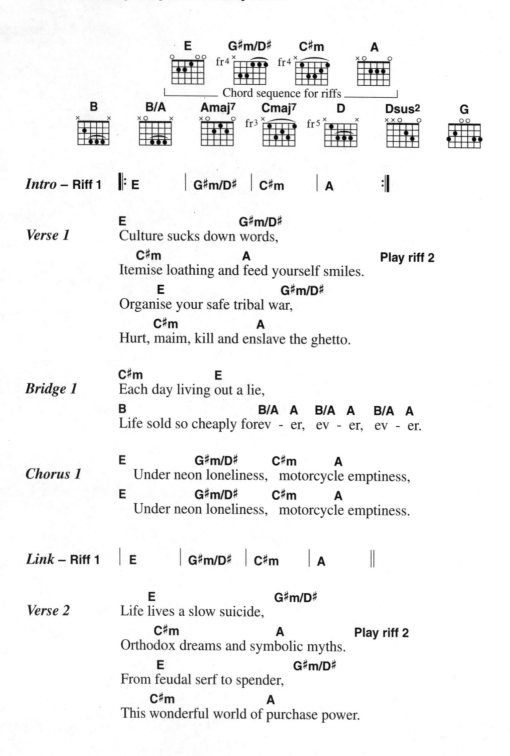

Intro – Riff 1 ‖: E | G♯m/D♯ | C♯m | A :‖

Verse 1

E G♯m/D♯
Culture sucks down words,

C♯m A Play riff 2
Itemise loathing and feed yourself smiles.

E G♯m/D♯
Organise your safe tribal war,

C♯m A
Hurt, maim, kill and enslave the ghetto.

Bridge 1

C♯m E
Each day living out a lie,

B B/A A B/A A B/A A
Life sold so cheaply forev - er, ev - er, ev - er.

Chorus 1

E G♯m/D♯ C♯m A
Under neon loneliness, motorcycle emptiness,

E G♯m/D♯ C♯m A
Under neon loneliness, motorcycle emptiness.

Link – Riff 1 | E | G♯m/D♯ | C♯m | A ‖

Verse 2

E G♯m/D♯
Life lives a slow suicide,

C♯m A Play riff 2
Orthodox dreams and symbolic myths.

E G♯m/D♯
From feudal serf to spender,

C♯m A
This wonderful world of purchase power.

Music by James Dean Bradfield & Sean Moore
© Copyright 1992 Sony/ATV Music Publishing (UK) Limited,
10 Great Marlborough Street, London W1.
All Rights Reserved. International Copyright Secured.

Bridge 2

C#m   E
Just like lungs sucking on air,

  B   B/A A B/A A B/A A
Survival's natural as sor - row, sor - row, sor - row.

Chorus 2

E   G#m/D# C#m A
 Under neon loneliness, motorcycle emptiness,

E   G#m/D# C#m A
 Under neon loneliness, motorcycle emptiness.

Picking | Amaj7 | B | Amaj7 | B | Cmaj7 | D | Cmaj7 | Dsus2 ||

Middle

Amaj7   B   Amaj7 B
All we want from you are the kicks you've given us,

Cmaj7   D   Cmaj7 D
All we want from you are the kicks you've given us,

Amaj7   B   Amaj7 B
All we want from you are the kicks you've given us,

Cmaj7   D   Cmaj7 Dsus2
All we want from you are the kicks you've given us.

Chorus 3

E   G#m/D# C#m A
 Under neon loneliness, motorcycle emptiness,

E   G#m/D# C#m A
 Under neon loneliness, motorcycle emptiness.

Solo | E | G | A | E | E | G | A | A ||

Verse 3

E   G#m/D#
Drive away and it's the same,

 C#m   A
Everywhere's death row, everyone's a victim.

  E   G#m/D#
Your joys are counterfeit,

 C#m   A
This happiness corrupt political shit.

Bridge 3

C#m   E
Living life like a comatose,

B   B/A A B/A A B/A A
Ego loaded and swal - low, swal - low, swal - low.

Chorus 4

  E   G#m/D# C#m A
||: Under neon loneliness, motorcycle emptiness,

E   G#m/D# C#m A
 Under neon loneliness, motorcycle emptiness. :|| *Repeat to fade*

8 Nothing Else Matters

May 1992 No. 6

IF YOU'D NEVER heard of Metallica before this 1992 single, you wouldn't have guessed that their origins were as a speed metal act whose biggest influence was Mötorhead! This chart-friendly ballad was taken off their number 1 album from the previous year, simply entitled *Metallica* (known to fans as 'The Black Album').

▼ E natural minor scale

Rhythm tips
Like many guitar classics, the idea behind 'Nothing Else Matters' is simple – twin guitarists Kirk Hammett and James Hetfield are picking E minor chords, one note at a time (see tab). Although the fingerstyle intro is fairly difficult for novice players, the basic accompaniment can be approximated by simply picking chords of Em, D and C. More adventurous players might like to try the slightly trickier D, Dsus4 and Cadd9 change that first appears in the second bar of the verses.

Layered guitars
Despite the simplistic chord sequence, the guitars on the original recording (and on our CD 'soundalike' version) are very carefully put together. There are two clean electric guitar parts, each with a light chorus effect, an acoustic guitar with reverb, and two distorted lead guitar lines, which occasionally play in harmony with each other. Improvising over a track as busy as 'Nothing Else Matters' isn't easy, but if you want to give it a try, we suggest you start with the E Natural Minor scale fretbox shown. You should be able to make up a credible solo whether you use a clean or dirty sound.

To play the clean rhythm part, use a bright guitar pickup setting (try the bridge pickup with the tone up full) and try reducing the middle control of the amp slightly. If you're using effects, set up your rig for compression, chorus and medium-length reverb.

Fascinating fact
Metallica are one of the few heavy metal acts to have a classical tribute band. Apocolyptica are four 'cellists from Finland who recorded an album called *Metallica by Four 'Cellos*. This actually *is* as weird as it sounds!

▼ Verse picking accompaniment

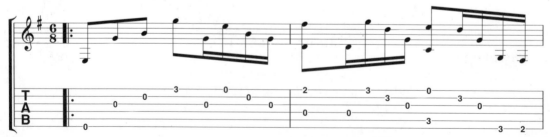

"We definitely put 110 per cent into this one, and that's what we got out."
James Hetfield

8 Nothing Else Matters

Words & Music by James Hetfield & Lars Ulrich

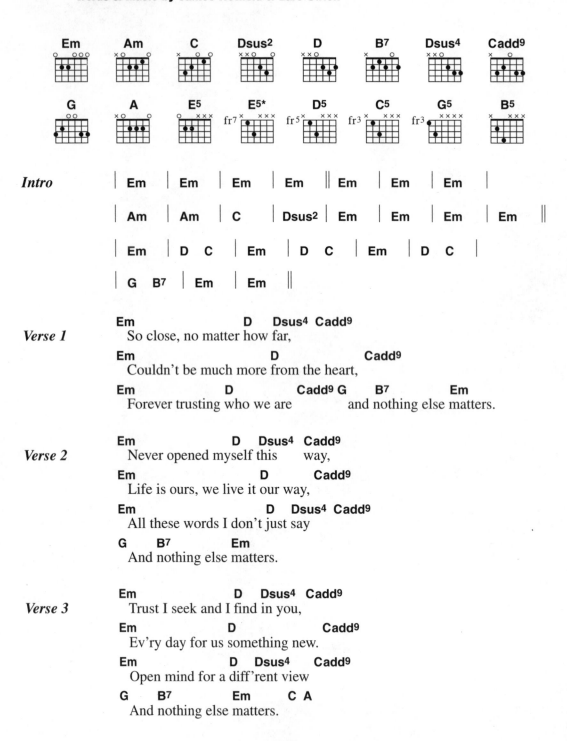

Intro

| Em | Em | Em | Em || Em | Em | Em |

| Am | Am | C | Dsus2 | Em | Em | Em | Em ||

| Em | D C | Em | D C | Em | D C |

| G B7 | Em | Em ||

Verse 1

Em   D   Dsus4 Cadd9
So close, no matter how far,

Em   D   Cadd9
Couldn't be much more from the heart,

Em   D   Cadd9 G   B7   Em
Forever trusting who we are   and nothing else matters.

Verse 2

Em   D   Dsus4 Cadd9
Never opened myself this   way,

Em   D   Cadd9
Life is ours, we live it our way,

Em   D   Dsus4 Cadd9
All these words I don't just say

G   B7   Em
And nothing else matters.

Verse 3

Em   D   Dsus4 Cadd9
Trust I seek and I find in you,

Em   D   Cadd9
Ev'ry day for us something new.

Em   D   Dsus4   Cadd9
Open mind for a diff'rent view

G   B7   Em   C A
And nothing else matters.

Chorus 1

    D   **C**   **A**
    Never cared for what they do,
    D   **C**   **A**
    Never cared for what they know,
    D   **Em**
    Oh, but I know.

Verse 4   As Verse 1

Chorus 2   As Chorus 1

Instrumental ‖: **Em** | **Em** | **Am** | **Am** | **C** | **Cadd9** | **Em** | **Em** :‖

Verse 5   As Verse 2

Verse 6   As Verse 3

Chorus 3

    D   **C**   **A**
    Never cared for what they say,
    D   **C**   **A**
    Never cared for games they play,
    D   **C**   **A**
    Never cared for what they do,
    D   **C**   **A**
    Never cared for what they know,
    D   **Em**
    Oh and I know, yeah, yeah.

Solo | **E5** | **D5** **C5** | **E5** | **D5** **C5** | **E5** | **D5** **C5** |

    | **G5** **B5** | **E5** | **E5** | **E5** | **E5** ‖

Verse 7

    Em   **D**   **Dsus4** **Cadd9**
    So close, no matter how far,
    Em   **D**   **Cadd9**
    Couldn't be much more from the heart,
    Em   **D**   **Dsus4** **Cadd9**
    Forever trusting who we are.
    G   **B7**   **Em**
    No, nothing else matters.

Outro   ‖: **Em** | **Em** | **Em** | **Em** | **Em** :‖ *Repeat to fade*

9 Parklife

September 1994 No. 10

BLUR'S THIRD TOP 10 hit featured the now-expected social comment from lyricist Damon Albarn, but guitarist Graham Coxon ensured that there were still riffs aplenty in the track. There are three main guitar sections – the main verse riff (E-A-Asus2); the low E bass string riff from the start of each chorus; and the picked arpeggio at the end of the chorus. All these are shown in the tab and fretboxes below, so it should be a simple matter to put the three together using the chord sheet provided.

▼ End of chorus arpeggio chord shape

The three riffs

That opening E chord part is doubled on two electric guitars in different octaves. The fretboxes show the high (12th fret) versions of the chords. Maintain the open strings notated in the fretboxes and you'll get close to the twin guitar effect of the original. The second riff is played as shown in the tab using alternating up and down strokes with the plectrum. The arpeggio at the end of the chorus (see chord above) can be picked in whatever direction feels comfortable, but make sure you hold the whole chord down so that the notes ring into one another.

The guitar tone is a slightly distorted bridge pickup sound, with reverb on each guitar. You will find that you can vary the tone (e.g. for the bass string riff) by picking very close to the bridge for a brighter sound.

Fascinating fact

'Parklife' was the first Blur single to feature a guest artist in the form of actor Phil Daniels, who supplied the spoken verse sections. Phil's other contributions to rock history include his appearances in The Who's film *Quadrophenia* and Hazel O'Connor's 'Breaking Glass'.

▼ Intro riff

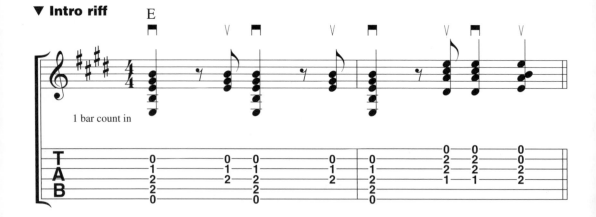

1 bar count in

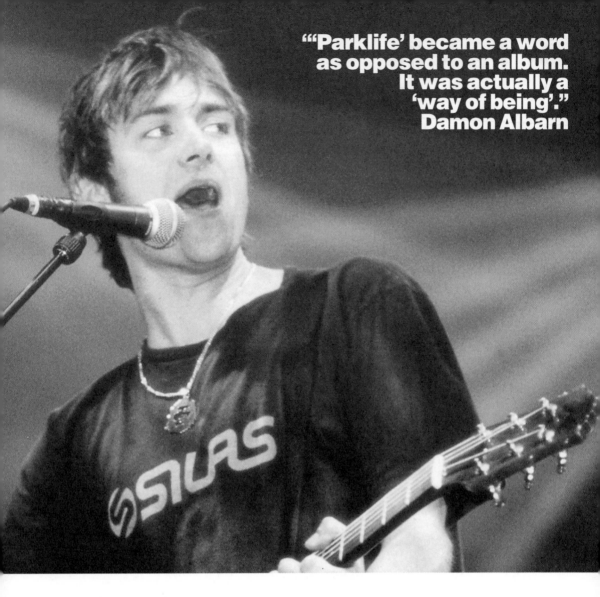

"'Parklife' became a word as opposed to an album. It was actually a 'way of being'."
Damon Albarn

▼ **Start of chorus riff**

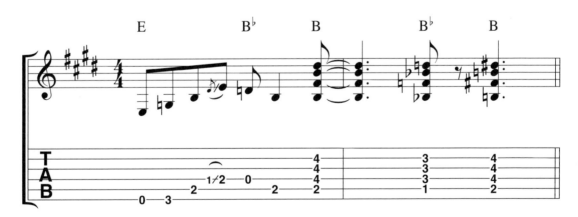

9 Parklife

Words & Music by Damon Albarn, Graham Coxon, Alex James & David Rowntree

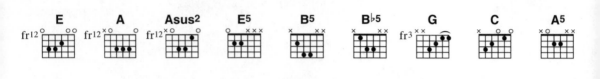

| E | A | Asus² | E⁵ | B⁵ | B♭5 | G | C | A⁵ |

Intro   ‖: E | E   A   Asus² :‖   *Play 6 times*

Verse 1

E
Confidence is a preference

         A   Asus²
For the habitual voyeur

     E   A   Asus²
Of what is known as parklife.

E
And morning soup can be avoided

       A   Asus² E
If you take a route straight through

       A   Asus²
What is known as parklife.

E
John's got brewer's droop,

        A   Asus² E
He gets intimidated by the dirty pigeons,

        A   Asus²
They love a bit of it, parklife.

E
Who's that gut lord marching,

       A   Asus² E
You should cut down on your porklife, mate,

        A   Asus²
Get some exercise.

Chorus 1

E⁵ B♭5 B⁵
All the people,

E⁵ B♭5 B⁵
So many people,

     G
They all go hand in hand,

C   A⁵ B♭5 B⁵
Hand in hand through their parklife.

Instrumental | E | E   A Asus² | E | E   A E |

Verse 2

E
I get up when I want

       A
Except on Wednesday

   Asus² E   **A**   **Asus²**
When I get rudely awakened by the dustmen (parklife).

E
I put my trousers on,

     A   **Asus²**
Have a cup of tea

     E   **A**   **Asus²**
And I think about leaving the house (parklife).

E
I feed the pigeons,

      A   **Asus²**
I sometimes feed the sparrows too,

E   **A**   **Asus²**
It gives me a sense of enormous well-being (parklife),

E
And then I'm happy for the rest of the day,

A   **Asus²**   **E**
Safe in the knowledge that there will always be

            A   **Asus²**
A bit of my heart devoted to it.

Chorus 2   As Chorus 1

E   **A**   **Asus² E**   **A**   **Asus²**
      Parklife,   (parklife),

E   **A**   **Asus² E**   **A**   **Asus²**
      Parklife,   (parklife).

E
It's got nothing to do with your

                  A   **Asus²**
Vorsprung durch technic, you know

E
And it's not about your joggers

               A   **Asus²**
Who go round and round and round.

Chorus 3   As Chorus 1

         Repeat to fade

Pick A Part That's New

May 1999 No. 4

JUST WHEN YOU THINK you can't do anything interesting with A, D and E, along comes a great riff that makes you wish you'd thought of it.

'Pick A Part That's New' uses a simple double-stopped idea, combining high fretted notes with open bass strings (see tab). Classic artists such as Chuck Berry and U2 have used this technique, but guitarist Kelly Jones uses a strumming style that owes more to Oasis, giving a '90s sound to the song.

The main riff

As with any double-stopped riff, correct string-muting technique is essential if you're going to avoid unwanted open strings from sounding. As you fret the notes shown in the tab, rest the remaining fingers of the fretting hand on the other strings lightly, just enough to prevent them from sounding. Keep your picking hand moving in a regular down-up motion (8 downstrokes to each bar) and you should find the rhythm of the upstrokes comes quite naturally.

How to get that sound

Kelly swears by his trusty Gibson SG – he says that since the Stereophonics became famous, Welsh music shops have never sold so many! Its high-output humbuckers, combined with overdrive from a Boss BD-2 and a valve amp, help to create the thick guitar sounds that characterise the band's work. For the rest of us, any middle-position pickup setting and medium overdrive setting should suffice, although Strat owners should try using higher overdrive settings and perhaps turning down the treble to compensate.

▼ Intro riff

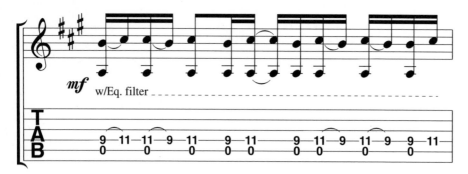

Kelly Jones' Gibson SG guitar is responsible for a large part of the Stereophonics' sound

10 Pick A Part That's New

Words by Kelly Jones. Music by Kelly Jones, Richard Jones & Stuart Cable

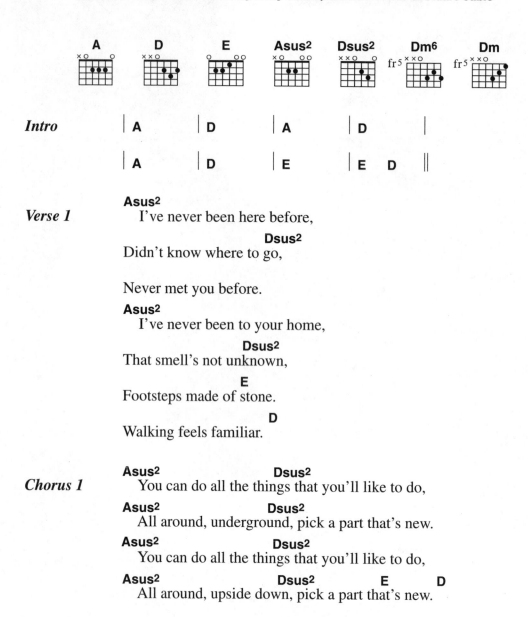

Intro

| A | D | A | D | |

| A | D | E | E D ||

Verse 1

Asus2
I've never been here before,

Dsus2
Didn't know where to go,

Never met you before.

Asus2
I've never been to your home,

Dsus2
That smell's not unknown,

E
Footsteps made of stone.

D
Walking feels familiar.

Chorus 1

Asus2   **Dsus2**
You can do all the things that you'll like to do,

Asus2   **Dsus2**
All around, underground, pick a part that's new.

Asus2   **Dsus2**
You can do all the things that you'll like to do,

Asus2   **Dsus2**   **E**   **D**
All around, upside down, pick a part that's new.

Verse 2

> **Asus²**
>
>   People drinking on their own,
>
>   **Dsus²**
>
> Push buttons on the phone,
>
> Was I here once before?
>
> **Asus²**
>
>   Is that my voice on the phone?
>
>   **Dsus²**
>
> That last drink on my own.
>
>   **E**
>
> Did I ever leave at all?
>
>   **D**
>
> Confusion's familiar.

Chorus 2   As Chorus 1

Solo

‖: A | A | Dm⁶ Dm | Dm⁶ Dm :‖

| E | E   D ‖

Chorus 3

> **Asus²**   **Dsus²**
>
>   You can do all the things that you'll like to do,
>
> **Asus²**   **Dsus²**
>
>   All around, underground, pick a part that's new.
>
> **Asus²**   **Dsus²**
>
>   You can do all the things that you'll like to do,
>
> **Asus²**   **Dsus²**
>
>   All around, upside down, anything that's new.

Chorus 4

> **Asus²**   **Dsus²**
>
>   You can do all the things that you'll like to do,
>
> **Asus²**   **Dsus²**
>
>   All around, underground, pick a part that's new.
>
> **Asus²**   **Dsus²**
>
>   You can do all the things that you'll like to do,
>
> **Asus²**   **Dsus²**   **E**
>
>   All around, upside down, pick a part that's new.

Coda

> **E**
>
> So what's new to you?
>
> So what's new to you?
>
>   **D**   **A**
>
> What's new to you?

11 Supersonic

23 April 1994 No. 31

'SUPERSONIC' WAS Oasis' first single, and one of the stand-out tracks from their debut album *Definitely Maybe*. Musically, its 8-to-the-bar accompaniment style owes more to rock acts such as AC/DC and Status Quo than to Noel's beloved Beatles songbook, but back in 1994 it was an exciting introduction to the Oasis sound for the UK fans.

Rhythm guitar tips

Like other Oasis hits (e.g. 'Wonderwall', 'She's Electric'), the verse of 'Supersonic' is based on a two-bar loop. Here, it starts with F♯5 (sliding down two frets to open E5 and then repeating), with A and B chords in the following bar. The first bridge section uses the F♯5 and E5 again, but each chord is held on for a whole vocal line at a time. After a slightly tricky 4th fret C♯7 barre chord we're into the first chorus, which uses more straightforward open chord shapes.

The driving rock accompaniment style uses 8 downstrokes per bar – there are very few upstrokes in the whole song. Note that none of the '5' chords (also called power chords) include the first two or three strings – these should be muted with the side of the picking hand. Noel's guitar solo is a straightforward melody rather than a spontaneous improvisation, and this is a good example of his melodic electric lead style. Each guitar solo is the same four-bar lick (see tab) repeated over the chords D-A5-E5-F♯5.

How to get that sound

The humbucker-through-Marshall Oasis sound is similar whichever guitar Noel chooses (he's normally associated with Epiphone semis, but has been seen with Les Pauls and a variety of other Gibsons). To set up your own guitar tone, select a thick overdrive with plenty of midrange (ideally using an amp – Oasis generally avoid multi-FX units), then add a more-than-average dose of reverb. If you're playing the song with another guitarist, remember that second guitarist Bonehead always played barre chords, while Noel played open chords.

▼ Guitar solo

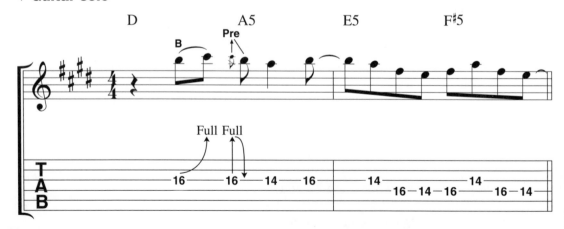

Supersonic

Words & Music by Noel Gallagher

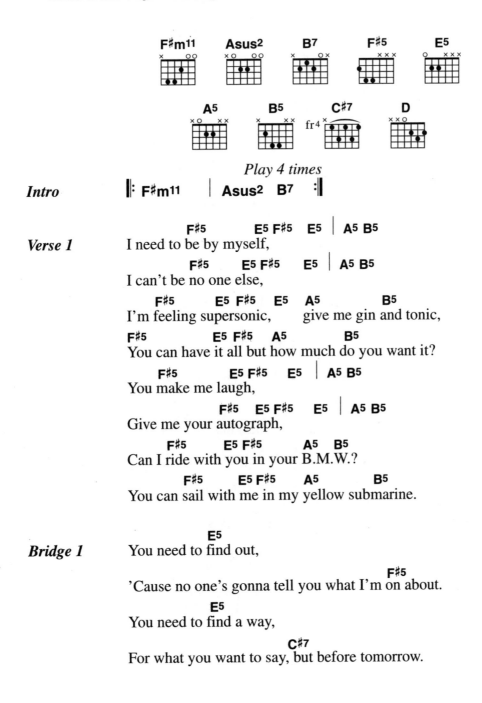

Play 4 times

Intro   ‖: F♯m¹¹ | Asus² B⁷   :‖

Verse 1

      F♯5   E5 F♯5 E5 | A5 B5
I need to be by myself,

      F♯5   E5 F♯5   E5 | A5 B5
I can't be no one else,

    F♯5   E5 F♯5 E5 A5   B5
I'm feeling supersonic,   give me gin and tonic,

F♯5   E5 F♯5 A5   B5
You can have it all but how much do you want it?

    F♯5   E5 F♯5 E5 | A5 B5
You make me laugh,

       F♯5 E5 F♯5   E5 | A5 B5
Give me your autograph,

    F♯5   E5 F♯5   A5 B5
Can I ride with you in your B.M.W.?

      F♯5   E5 F♯5   A5   B5
You can sail with me in my yellow submarine.

Bridge 1

      E5
You need to find out,

                    F♯5
'Cause no one's gonna tell you what I'm on about.

      E5
You need to find a way,

            C♯7
For what you want to say, but before tomorrow.

Supersonic

Chorus 1

       D   A5   E5   F#5
'Cause my friend said he'd take you home,

      D   A5   E5   F#5
He sits in a corner all alone.

D   A5   E5   F#5
He lives under a waterfall,

D   A5
Nobody can see him,

E5   F#5   D   A5
Nobody can ever hear him call,

E5   F#5   D   A5
Nobody can ever hear him call.

Guitar solo

| E5 F#5 | D A5 | E5 F#5 | D A5 |

| E5 F#5 | E5 | E5 | C#7 | C#7 |

Verse 2

             F#5   E5 F#5   E5 | A5 B5
You need to be yourself,

             F#5   E5 F#5   E5 | A5 B5
You can't be no one else.

   F#5   E5   F#5 E5   A5   B5
I know a girl called Elsa, she's into Alka Seltzer,

     F#5   E5 F#5   A5   B5
She sniffs it through a cane on a supersonic train.

        F#5   E5 F#5 E5 | A5 B5
And she makes me laugh,

         F#5 E5 F#5   E5 | A5 B5
I got her autograph.

      F#5   E5 F#5   E5 A5   B5
She's done it with a doctor   on a helicopter,

    F#5   E5 F#5   E5 A5   B5
She's sniffin' in her tissue, sellin' the big issue.

Bridge 2

         E5
When she finds out,

                           F#5
'Cause no ones's gonna tell her what I'm on about.

         E5
You need to find a way

             C#7
For what you want to say, but before tomorrow.

Chorus 2

D	A⁵	E⁵	F♯5

'Cause my friend said he'd take you home,

D	A⁵	E⁵	F♯5

He sits in a corner all alone.

D	A⁵	E⁵	F♯5

He lives under a waterfall,

D	A⁵

Nobody can see him,

E⁵	F♯5	D	A⁵

Nobody can ever hear him call,

E⁵	F♯5	D	A⁵

Nobody can ever hear him call.

Guitar solo ‖: E⁵ F♯5 │ D A⁵ :‖ *Repeat to fade*

12 Tears In Heaven

February 1992 No. 5

'TEARS IN HEAVEN' was written in memory of Eric Clapton's young son Connor, who died in 1991, and has become one of Clapton's most popular recordings. It appeared on the 1992 album *MTV Unplugged* which helped to maintain Clapton's status as the world's best-known guitar player.

Picking tips
The song is played on a nylon-strung acoustic, which, due to its lighter string tension, makes it considerably easier to play than on a regular steel-strung. It's also worth remembering that it's one of the most difficult songs to play in this book, especially if you're new to fingerstyle. So in short – don't get too disheartened if it doesn't sound right at first! The picking hand fingers should cover the first four strings, while the thumb picks the bass notes on the fifth and sixth strings. If you find it difficult to get the exact picking patterns, remember that the chords we've shown are the exact ones used on the original recording. This means that as long as you avoid picking any of the strings marked with an X, you should be able to devise a part that sounds close to the recorded version.

Easy version
If you still find the chords too difficult, remember that with 'slash' chord notation, the letter to the left of the slash refers to the chord, and the one to the right refers to the bass note. So for example, if your fingers can't manage the E/G♯, simply strum a regular E chord – this will sound fine when you play along to the CD.

Fascinating fact
In a 1999 poll, this song was voted number 3 in the Top 5 acoustic pieces played by guitarists in music shops. For the record, the others were The Beatles' 'Blackbird', Arlo Guthrie's 'Alice's Restaurant' and Oasis' 'Wonderwall'. Number 1, of course, was Led Zeppelin's 'Stairway to Heaven'.

▼ Intro picking riff

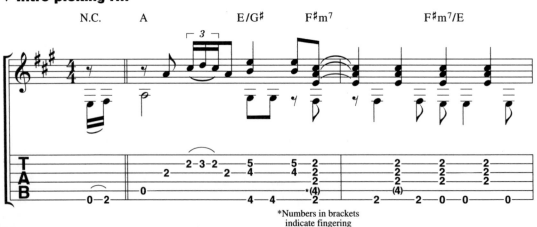

*Numbers in brackets
indicate fingering

Tears In Heaven

Words & Music by Eric Clapton & Will Jennings

A	E/G♯	F♯m7	F♯m7/E	D/F♯	E7sus4
E7	A/E	E	F♯m	C♯/E♯	A7/E	F♯7
Bm7	Bm7/E	C	G/B	Am	G	Em

(chord diagrams)

Intro | A   E/G♯ | F♯m7 F♯m7/E | D/F♯   E7sus4 E7 | A   ‖

Verse 1

A   E/G♯   F♯m7 F♯m7/E
Would I know your name

D/F♯ A/E   E
If I   saw you in heaven?

A   E/G♯ F♯m7 F♯m7/E
Would it be the same

D/F♯ A/E   E
If I   saw you in heaven?

Chorus 1

F♯m   C♯/E♯
I must be strong

A7/E   F♯7
  And carry on,

       Bm7   Bm7/E
'Cause I know I don't belong

     A
Here in heaven.

Link | A   E/G♯ | F♯m7 F♯m7/E | D/F♯   E7sus4 E7 | A   ‖

Verse 2

```
A          E/G♯    F♯m7  F♯m7/E
Would you hold my hand

D/F♯ A/E        E
If I   saw you in heaven?

A          E/G♯  F♯m7  F♯m7/E
Would you help me stand

D/F♯ A/E        E
If I   saw you in heaven?
```

Chorus 2

```
F♯m        C♯/E♯
I'll find my way

A7/E                F♯7
Through night and day

        Bm7              Bm7/E
'Cause I know I just can't stay

        A
Here in heaven.
```

Link

```
| A   E/G♯ | F♯m7  F♯m7/E | D/F♯  E7sus4  E7 | A        ||
```

Bridge

```
C       G/B        Am
Time can bring you down,

        D/F♯         G   D/F♯ Em D/F♯ G
Time can bend your knees.

C       G/B        Am
Time can break your heart,

        D/F♯       G    D/F♯
Have you beggin' please,

        E
Beggin' please.
```

Solo

```
||: A   E/G♯ | F♯m7  F♯m7/E | D/F♯  A/E | E   E7 :||
```

Chorus 3

```
F♯m        C♯/E♯
Beyond the door

A7/E                F♯7
There's peace I'm sure

        Bm7              Bm7/E
And I know there'll be no more

        A
Tears in heaven.
```

Verse 3

    A   **E/G♯**   **F♯m7** **F♯m7/E**
Would you know my name

D/F♯ A/E   **E**
If I   saw you in heaven?

    A   **E/G♯ F♯m7 F♯m7/E**
Would you be the same

D/F♯ A/E   **E**
If I   saw you in heaven?

Chorus 4

F♯m   **C♯/E♯**
I must be strong

A7/E   **F♯7**
And carry on,

          Bm7   **Bm7/E**
'Cause I know I don't belong

       A
Here in heaven.

Link

 | **A   E/G♯** | **F♯m7 F♯m7/E** ‖

          Bm7   **Bm7/E**
'Cause I know I don't belong

       A
Here in heaven.

Coda

 | **A E/G♯** | **F♯m7 F♯m7/E** | **A/E   E7sus4 E7** | **A** ‖

Ten Storey Love Song

March 1995 No. 11

THE STONE ROSES' John Squire has been called 'a guitar hero for the '90s' and 'a modern Jimmy Page' by the UK guitar press, and one listen to 'Ten Storey Love Song' should be enough to hear why. The song features lead guitar virtually all the way through, sometimes even doubling the vocal line.

▼ **D major scale (7th fret version)**

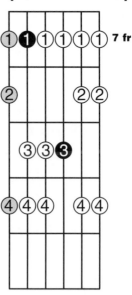

Acoustic guitar part

The novice player will be pleased to learn that underneath that busy lead guitar part are some nice easy chords. On the recording, these open chords of D, G etc (see fretboxes) are played on a 12-string acoustic, doubled by an electric guitar with a clean sound. Note that the chords aren't strummed all the time – at the start of each verse they're just played once at the beginning of each bar. Full rhythmic strumming starts when the band enters, in bar 4 of the verse (over "so much in love…"). Note also the D/F♯ chord – the bass note should be fretted with the thumb over the top of the neck. This is quite tricky to do, so if you can't manage it simply play a D chord and avoid hitting the two bottom strings.

Soloing tips

That melodic lead style is a result of John Squire's choice of scale. Many beginner rock players tend to play the minor pentatonic scale over *everything*, which unfortunately doesn't work in a major-key song like this. The melodic feel is generated by a combination of major scale use and careful phrasing (i.e. leaving gaps in between each phrase to let the music 'breathe', just like a vocalist). To help you to devise your own major-key melodies, we've shown the D major scale in one of John's favourite positions, and tabbed out the first part of the lead part from the chorus.

How to get that sound

The characteristic 'jangle' Roses' guitar sound is created using a combination of instrumentation (12-string doubling 6-string), production (bright, trebly guitar tones) and technique (using open chords rather than barre shapes). To duplicate this effect yourself, select the bridge pickup on your guitar, boost the treble on your amp, and add a very thick reverb. A chorus pedal and moderate overdrive will go some way towards recreating that twin-guitar effect.

Fascinating fact

The Stone Roses' arrogance in the '90s was legendary. Even their songs were conceited, with titles such as 'I Am The Resurrection' and 'I Wanna Be Adored'. After the release of their first album they refused to support *anyone*, even (allegedly) turning down a tour with The Rolling Stones.

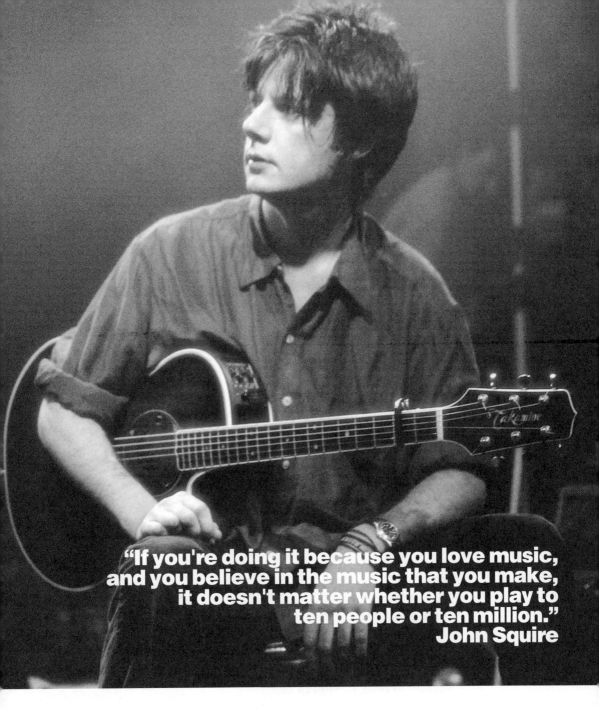

"If you're doing it because you love music, and you believe in the music that you make, it doesn't matter whether you play to ten people or ten million."
John Squire

▼ **Chorus lead guitar part**

13 Ten Storey Love Song

Words & Music by John Squire

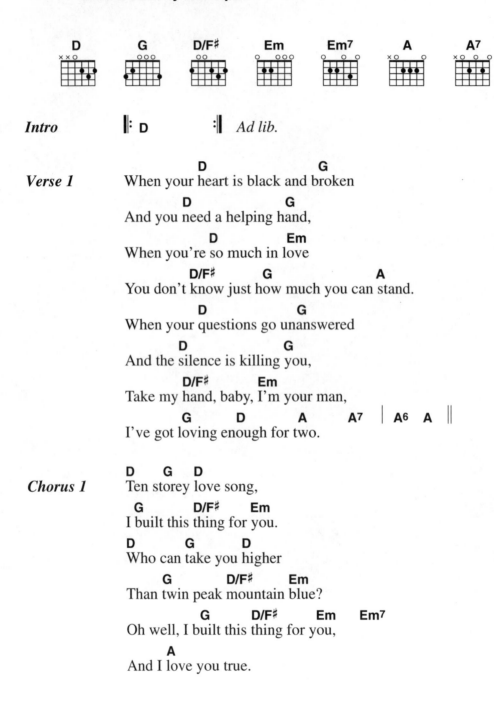

D   G   D/F#   Em   Em7   A   A7   A6

Intro   ‖: D   :‖ *Ad lib.*

Verse 1
                D   G
When your heart is black and broken
           D   G
And you need a helping hand,
              D   Em
When you're so much in love
             D/F#   G   A
You don't know just how much you can stand.
              D   G
When your questions go unanswered
           D   G
And the silence is killing you,
           D/F#   Em
Take my hand, baby, I'm your man,
           G   D   A   A7 | A6 A ‖
I've got loving enough for two.

Chorus 1
D   G   D
Ten storey love song,
 G   D/F#   Em
I built this thing for you.
D   G   D
Who can take you higher
        G   D/F#   Em
Than twin peak mountain blue?
           G   D/F#   Em   Em7
Oh well, I built this thing for you,
        A
And I love you true.

Verse 2

         D   **G**
There's no sure-fire set solutions,

        D   **G**
No short cut through the trees.

       D   **Em**
No breach in the wall that they

  D   **G**   **A**
Put there to keep you from me.

         D   **G**
As you're lying awake in this darkness,

       D   **G**
This everlasting night.

     D/F♯   **Em**
Someday soon, don't know where or when,

      G   **D/F♯** **A**   **A⁷** | **A⁶** **A** ‖
You're gonna wake up and see the light._____

Chorus 2

D **G** **D**
Ten storey love song,

 G   **D/F♯**   **Em**
I built this thing for you.

D   **G**   **D**
Who can take you higher

   G   **D/F♯**   **Em**
Than twin peak mountain blue?

    G   **D/F♯**   **Em**   **Em⁷**
Oh well, I built this thing for you,

    A
And I love you true.

Bridge

| **G** | **A** | **G** | **A** | **G** | **A**

| **G** **D/F♯** | **Em** **Em⁷** | **A** **A⁷** | **A⁶** **A** ‖

Chorus 3   As Chorus 2

Coda   ‖: **D**   :‖ *Ad lib. to fade*

September 1993 No. 14

THERE ARE VERY FEW songs that can be identified by their chords alone, but Paul Weller's acoustic-friendly 'Wild Wood' is a rare example. Simply play open Am, then take your third and first fingers off to create Em/A, then strum Dm7 and finally Dm7 with a flat 5 (easier than it sounds – see fretbox). That's all there is to it.

Keep it interesting
Obviously, when a song is based on a loop of only four chords, you need to work that bit harder to keep the audience listening. With this in mind, it's worth working out a few variations on the basic pattern. Start with a straight 'oom-pah' where you pluck the bass note followed by a brief down-strum of the top three strings. Then, as the verse develops, try following the downstroke with a brief upstroke to create the rhythmic 'swing' that drives the backing track. Combine these two ideas with regular up-down strumming patterns and you'll be able to use the picking style to vary the dynamics of the track.

▼ B blues scale

Taking a solo
On the original recording (and our 'soundalike' CD version) the guitar solo is closely based on the main melody. Use the B blues scale (see fretbox) to work out the tune of the actual solo, or make up your own improvisation. Listen carefully to the fourth chord of the loop when you're soloing – not every scale note will sound right for this bar of music.

Capo techniques
If you're going to play along with the CD you'll need a capo at the 2nd fret. If you don't own one you'll have to use your first finger to barre the 2nd fret, but this will be difficult, and the ringing tone of the capo'd notes will be lost. You could just about get away with tuning the guitar up to F♯-B-E-A-C♯-F♯, but you're seriously increasing your chances of string breakage. Just buy a capo, OK?

▼ Intro rhythm pattern

∏ = downstroke   V = upstroke

"There's definitely something about my songs when they're led by my voice and guitar. They grab people... I guess that's what I was reminded of... what I used to get out of music."
Paul Weller

14 Wild Wood

Words & Music by Paul Weller

Am   Em/A   Dm7   Dm7♭5/E

Capo second fret

Intro

| Am | Am | Em/A | Em/A | |
| Dm7 | Dm7♭5/E | Am | Am | ‖

Verse 1

Am   Em/A
High tide, mid-afternoon,

Dm7   Dm7♭5/E   Am
People fly by   in the   traffic's boom.

                    Em/A
Knowing just where you're blowing,

Dm7   Dm7♭5/E   Am
Getting to where   you should be going.

Verse 2

Am   Em/A
Don't let them get you down,

Dm7   Dm7♭5/E   Am
Making you feel   guilty about

                  Em/A
Golden rain will bring you   riches,

Dm7   Dm7♭5/E   Am
All the good things   you deserve now.

Solo

| Am | Am | Em/A | Em/A | |
| Dm7 | Dm7♭5/E | Am | Am | ‖

Verse 3

Am   **Em/A**
Climbing, forever   trying,

Dm7   **Dm7♭5/E**   **Am**
Find your way out   of the   wild, wild wood.

                 Em/A
Now there's no   justice,

       Dm7   **Dm7♭5/E**   **Am**
You've only yourself   that you can trust in.

Verse 4

Am   **Em/A**
And I said, high tide mid-afternoon,

       Dm7   **Dm7♭5/E**   **Am**
Woah, people fly by   in the   traffic's boom.

                Em/A
Knowing just where you're blowing,

Dm7   **Dm7♭5/E**   **Am**
Getting to where   you should be going.

Solo

| **Am** | **Am** | **Em/A** | **Em/A** |

| **Dm7** | **Dm7♭5/E** | **Am** | **Am** ‖

Verse 5

Am   **Em/A**
Day by day your world fades away,

Dm7   **Dm7♭5/E**   **Am**
Waiting to feel   all the   dreams that say

                 Em/A
Golden rain will bring you   riches,

Dm7   **Dm7♭5/E** **Am**
All the good things   you deserve now, and I say,

Verse 6

Am   **Em/A**
Climbing, forever trying,

           Dm7   **Dm7♭5/E** **Am**
You're gonna find your way out   of the   wild, wild wood.

            Em/A   **Dm7♭5/E**
I said you're gonna find your way out

      Am
Of the wild, wild wood.

15 Zombie

October 1994 No. 14

IF YOU'VE BEEN having trouble with some of the more challenging songs in this book, then 'Zombie' should come as a welcome relief. Cranberries singer-songwriter Dolores O'Riordan doesn't try to be a guitar hero, and is often content to play simple open chords to let her distinctive vocal shine through.

Accompaniment styles

Like 'Wild Wood' and 'Supersonic', 'Zombie' is based on a four-chord repeated pattern of Em-Cmaj7-G6-G6/F♯. In the intro, this is played using a clean electric guitar sound, simply strumming the chords lightly with a plectrum. Next, the band enters, and the bass plays 8-to-the-bar downstrokes along with Noel Hogan's fuzzed-up barre chords. For the vocal sections, the clean electric part is arpeggiated, i.e. picked one note at a time.

Soloing tips

The guitar solo uses the E natural minor scale played in parallel 4ths. If this sounds too technical, take a look at the scale shape in the tab. The whole solo is played by fretting the first two strings with the first finger at the 7th fret, and then simply sliding it around the positions shown.

How to get that sound

The clean electric guitar part uses an in-between pickup position, with reverb and chorus added. The chorus speed should be set ultra-slow (about two cycles a second) to achieve a flanger-like effect. For the full-band sections, simply select the bridge pickup and pile on as much distortion as you like!

▼ **Finger positions for guitar solo**

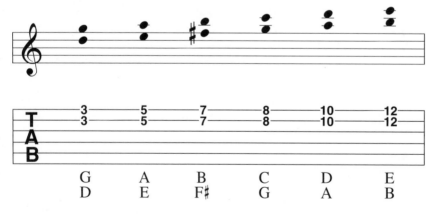

"Pretty much as soon as I started playing
I had this dream of playing forever...
that's what I wanted to do because it was the
only thing that I was actually good at
and felt confident doing."
Noel Hogan

15 Zombie

Words & Music by Dolores O'Riordan

Em · Cmaj7 · G6 · G6/F#

Intro   ‖: Em | Cmaj7 | G6 | G6/F# :‖ *Play 4 times*

Verse 1

Em   Cmaj7
Another head hangs lowly,
G6   G6/F#
Child is slowly taken.
Em   Cmaj7
And the violence caused such silence,
G6   G6/F#
Who are we mistaken?

        Em
But you see, it's not me,

        Cmaj7
It's not my family,

      G6
In your head, in your head,

       G6/F#
They are fighting.

        Em
With their tanks and their bombs

       Cmaj7
And their bombs and their guns,

      G6   G6/F#
In your head, in your head they are crying.

Chorus 1

      Em   Cmaj7
In your head, in your head,
    G6   G6/F#
Zombie, zombie, zombie, hey, hey.

        Em   Cmaj7
What's in your head, in your head?
    G6   G6/F#
Zombie, zombie, zombie, hey, hey, hey.

Bridge 1

       Em   **Cmaj7**
Oh, doo, doo, doo, doo,

               G6
Doo, doo, doo, doo,

             G6/F♯
Doo, doo, doo, doo,

          Em **Cmaj7** **G6** **G6/F♯**
Doo, doo, doo, doo.

Verse 2

Em   **Cmaj7**   **G6**
  Another mother's breakin' heart

       G6/F♯
Is taking over.

Em   **Cmaj7**
  When the violence causes silence,

G6   **G6/F♯**
We must be mistaken.

           Em
It's the same old theme

          Cmaj7
Since nine - teen sixteen,

     G6
In your head, in your head,

         G6/F♯
They're still fighting.

         Em
With their tanks and their bombs

       Cmaj7
And their bombs and their guns,

     G6   **G6/F♯**
In your head, in your head they are dying.

Chorus 2   As Chorus 1

Bridge 2

Em
Oh, oh, oh, oh,

Cmaj7
Oh, oh, oh, hey,

G6   **G6/F♯**
Oh, ya, ya.

Instrumental | Em | Cmaj7 | G6 | G6/F♯ ‖: Em | Cmaj7 | Em | Cmaj7 :‖

Solo   ‖: Em | Cmaj7 | G6 | G6/F♯ :‖ *Play 4 times*

         | Em | Cmaj7 | Em | Cmaj7 | Em | Cmaj7 | Em ‖

Further Reading

If you've enjoyed this book why not check out some of the great titles below. They are available from all good music retailers and book shops, or you can visit our website: www.musicsales.com. In case of difficulty please contact Music Sales direct (see page 2).

The Chord Songbook Series

Play all your favourite hits with just a few easy chords for each song! Huge range of titles to choose from, including:

NEW! **Abba** AM959740
The Beatles NO90664
Blur AM936914
Bon Jovi AM936892
Boyzone AM956956
Eric Clapton AM956054
The Corrs AM956967
The Cranberries AM944383
The Levellers AM951445
Metallica AM944680
Alanis Morissette AM944086
Oasis AM936903
Oasis 2 AM951478
Pulp AM942678
Stereophonics AM956065

Sting AM940489
Stone Roses AM951500
Paul Weller AM942546
Wet Wet Wet AM938135
The Who AM956021

Play Guitar With...Series

Play guitar and sing along with the specially-recorded CD backing tracks for classic songs from your favourite bands. Here are just some of the titles in this superb series.

The Beatles NO90665
The Beatles Book 2 NO90667
The Beatles Book 3 NO90689
Blur AM935320
Bon Jovi AM92558
Eric Clapton AM950862

The Kinks AM951863
Kula Shaker AM943767
Metallica AM92559
Alanis Morissette AM943723
Oasis AM935330
Ocean Colour Scene AM943712
Stereophonics AM
Sting AM928092
The Stone Roses AM943701

...plus many more titles for you to collect!